CW00456934

My Vibrating Vertebrae

and other poems

A M Graham

Copyright © 2016 C Graham & L J Baker

Published by C Graham & L J Baker

No part of this book may be reproduced in any form, including electronic, without written permission from the publishers, except for brief quotations for review purposes.

This is a work of fiction.

Any resemblance to real characters, places, or events, is purely coincidental.

Acknowledgements:

Editing & Formatting by

Jo Robinson Indie Author Support Services

Cover Design by

C Graham TSRA Book Covers

Using purchased Standard License images from

chachar / 123RF Stock Photo

&

basel101658 / 123RF Stock Photo

In Loving Memory of our Mother

Our Mum, Agnes Mae Graham, enjoyed making up poetry to express her thoughts, a talent she inherited from her Father, William James Lennon, but seems to have omitted passing the talent on to my sister or me, so I'm grateful that after Mum's death my sister Lorna kept all Mum's poems that she could find. Sadly, our Grandfather's poems had long since been lost.

The poems in this small book are not in any particular order, but they span decades of Mum's life in Northern Ireland, and cover a range of thoughts including humour, sadness, and in one case the downright nonsensical.

Please note that words marked* are explained at the end of the book.

Contents

My Homeland

The six counties of Ulster,

are ever on my mind.

For now I must leave them,

so very, very far behind.

First love is County Antrim,

where I first saw the light of day.

In Larne my first glimpse of the sea,

was from the beach of Sandy Bay.

Then second love, sweet County Down,

we lived there long after we wed.

Beloved coast from Holywood,

to well past Newcastle Head.

Fermanagh with its Loughs of Erne,

many holidays we there spent.

By car, by bus, yea by boat,

as o'er land and lough we went.

Londonderry, county of wars,

of weeping, and of travail.

Yet such beauty in the turn,

of river and green of vale.

Wee Tyrone among the bushes,

a Sylvania for the eyes of delight.

Sure there's forty shades of green,

you'll see by summers light.

Armagh, the orchard county,

of apple, of plum, of pear.

The scent of Heaven's glory land,

from blossoms waft the air.

Yes, my air, my own brave Ulster,

God grant that you are free.

That I may return to my wee home,

for Ulster is Home Sweet Home to me.

William John McQuade

Did you ever hear the story William John McQuade?

He was well known as the laziest man in Larne.

He'd sit before the fire until he'd smoke and singe,

then call his ma, 'Ma turn me or I'll burn'.

Once Ma boiled his spuds in their skins,

then put a knife and fork where he could see,

called 'Your dinner's ready my wee son'.

He answered 'Spuds not peeled, then I'll wait for tea'.

Once she went to market, one Wednesday morn in March,

to buy her son a cushion, and the hearth a nice new fender,

when neighbours met her with the news,

with no ma to turn him, William John burnt down to a cinder.

So all you doting mothers, with a great big lazy son,

be warned!! Sure a pile o' ashes is no use to anyone.

Jessie

There was a little girl everyone abhorred,

she was very naughty, and always slamming doors.

Please go out quietly dear, her poor mummy called,

you'll wake up Grandad, and out of bed he'll fall.

But Jessie doesn't listen, she bangs the door and goes,

poor Mummy dropped the iron on her tender toes.

Every day when Jessie came in or went out,

she banged and banged till Mummy near passed out.

But one day, she went into Father's special den,

she banged the door; a big lion's head fell down on her just then.

So now poor Jessie slams no more doors or so it's said,

the big lion's head knocked Jessie out – she's dead!!

Rosie and Willie

'I was thinking of getting married, Rosie me love,

but before you say yes, wait and tell.

Can you do all the things a good wife can do,

aye, Rosie me love, and do well?'

'Can ye bake soda bread, Rosie me love,

can ye turn a chop in the pan.

Can ye make Irish stew or a meat pie,

turn a griddle of fadge*, say ye can?!'

She looked at her lily white hands,

as she bowed her pretty head,

then she blushed as she looked up and said,

'No, Willie, I can't, oh Willie I can't, but me Ma can!'

'Can ye milk a fine cow, Rosie me love,

can ye rear a good litter and sow.

Can ye set broody hens, and rear their chicks,

can ye yoke a carthorse to a plough?'

She looked at her lily white hands,

as she bowed her pretty head,

then she blushed as she looked up and said,

'No, Willie, I can't, oh Willie I can't, but me Ma can!'

'Can ye sew a fine seam, Rosie me love,

can ye turn a shirt collar trim an' neat.

Can ye knit thick socks, turn a Dutch heel,

to keep me warm about the feet?'

She looked at her lily white hands,

as she bowed her pretty head,

then she blushed as she looked up and said,

'No, Willie, I can't, oh Willie I can't, but me Ma can!'

'When can we be married, Willie me love,

make it soon, or I'll die with the sorrow.

I'll wear a white gown, and paint up me face,

Oh Willie love, I can marry you tomorrow.'

He looked at his work worn hands,

and he smiled as he looked up and said,

'No, ye canny, no Rosie ye can't,

but your ma can.'

Kitty and Joe

Just six months before our Ulster strife began,

Kitty Boyle, a Catholic, married Joe Dunn, an Orangeman.

It was a romantic wedding, they eloped to Gretna Green.

Joe was tall and twenty, Kitty small and seventeen.

The love in their hearts was shining in their eyes for all to see,

as hand in hand together, they walked in Ulster free.

Then the 'Troubles' started, and overnight it seems,

the first bomb was thrown and shattered all their dreams.

Instead of *my darling Kitty,* and *my beloved Joe,*

it was you're a Prod* Joey, you're a Fenian* Kitty, and parted so.

Kitty wore a black beret, and fought with bomb and gun.

Joe joined Vigilantes to fight the Fenian* Hun.

Oh, dear Lord, what's happened to youth of birth,

from love to hate, just overnight, to give the devil mirth.

Then it happened, the Catholic fighting Prods,

hand to hand, with knife and brick, each calling to their Gods.

Joe looked up and Kitty too, each other they were fighting,

love turned to hate, no chance of them righting.

A flash of blade from two right hands it was done,

no more kisses, no more love, no more harmless fun.

The two lay dead side by side, each the other blighted,

Kitty and Joe, in life apart, in death's dark vale united.

God grant that such poor mortals, as Joe and Kitty Dunn,

shall like our Lord, forgive them, they know not what they have done.

Memories of the Old Mayfair

I sat down with a gasp on the settee,

I was tired, I was beat and I sighed.

All was papered, whitened and curtains made clean,

all the ceilings and the paintwork nearly dried.

The sun shone through the window pane,

and I realised with a start of dismay,

the date of the month, the day of the week.

It was Tuesday the twenty-first of May.

My heart gladdened as I now recalled,

ten years ago, when I was just sixteen.

The Ballyclare Mayfair, was to my young heart,

something to plan for, to wish and to dream.

Two of my pals and I went that year,

best cotton dresses and ribbons in our hair.

We cycled three abreast ('Tis a crime ye know),

full of joy, with half–crown each to spare.

We left our three bikes at a house on the way,

and started on the walk into the town.

A mile to be sure, but we didn't care,

anticipation made us laugh and never frown.

We giggled and blushed, and tittered with glee,

as three young lads, behind us we espied.

Soon they hastened their steps, and do ye know,

there they were, just by chance, by our side.

We soon paired off, the three lads and we.

Mine was a big braw lad name of Paul,

I've never walked such a very short mile,

all too soon we were at the Town Hall.

We went on the swings and the chair-o-planes,

the steam ships for us held no fear.

We screamed our way round on the ocean wave,

then tried our luck with the darts for a dare.

We bought yellow man and ate hard nuts,

they are treats far beyond compare.

We went to a tea room and ate six plain teas,

it was better than all your grand fare.

Soon it was eight, time for the dance,

so off we went to the old Abbey Hall.

We got in okay but boy was it full,

if you tripped, you had nae* room to fall.

We stood near the door, as the chairs were all full,

then we danced to the fiddler's fine tune.

It was better, it was gayer than any fine ball,

but, oh gosh, it was over too soon.

To dance in that crush was a grand excuse,

to cuddle your partner, e'er so tight.

Cheek to cheek, we all shuffled in ecstasy,

then twelve o'clock and it was midnight.

We walked along that dark and lonely road,

three pairs of young folks, holding hands.

We were subdued as we neared the house,

where the boys got our bikes from the stands.

We sadly clasped our hands, and kissed farewell,

(My first lovers' kiss I now confess).

We cycled off, all reluctant to part,

three, now quiet girls, our thoughts you can guess.

Ballyclare Mayfair, oh can you wonder now,

with what joy, as that day recall.

The tears come to my eyes even yet,

for that tall dark farmer's lad named Paul.

Wake up now, dreamin' may be done,

but the tea is still to be had.

For my two hungry sons, and a hungry man,

yes, my own, my braw* Ballycastle lad.

The Lealies

In a wee place called Kilwaughter,

just three miles out o' Larne,

is a town land called 'The Lealies',

where my ain* Da was born.

When I was wee and full 'o fun,

I'd go there wi' my faither*,

my two sisters, and mammy too,

we'd walk there using leather.

Uncle Eddie and his wife Mary,

would gi' us all a welcome greetin',

for good friends all, a welcome warm,

Aye was a pleasure meetin'.

Aunt Mary's girls, three in all,

Nance, Ellie and wee baby Pearl.

Two sons as well, Tommy the lad,

Scott, handsomer than any girl.

The five o' them, the three o' us,

A noisy band of happy fun.

In hay-sheds, through the byres,

we'd make the poor hens run.

Good home baked soda farls* we ate,

and treacle scones and tattie breed.

Nae* fancy icing cakes to us,

was e'er welcomed more than this homely feed.

Now all are far and widely flung,

Aunt Mary, Mother, Ellie and Nance.

And sister Essie, all gone home,

no more shoutin' or farmyard dance.

Uncle Eddie is now sick and old,

Dad 's still fresh but all alone.

Tommy owns a garage on the Doagh Road,

Pearl made Australia her present home.

My one sister in Larne left still,

at the top o' the new Craigyhill,

Only Scott our wee handsome pet,

now married lives in 'the Lealies' yet.

Myself, I'm away in County Down,

New home, new friends, I've gathered round.

But sure you'll forgive, if a tear I shed,

for Lealies, for friends, for youth long dead.

Journey in an Aeroplane

Were you ever in an aeroplane?

My, but the feelings are hard to ponder.

The engine starts, the speed builds up,

then you're in the blue yonder.

We boarded the plane at Aldergrove,

and up the steps we staggered.

Our hearts in our mouths, our faces white,

our eyes all looking haggard.

300 miles an hour 9,000 feet up,

the fields looked so wee and neat.

The roads like grey ribbons,

and the houses like those for dolls, so petite.

The rivers were like silver bands,

the trees like chips of green jade.

A lough, like a shimmering jewel lay,

what precious things our God has made.

Clouds now each side like fleecy snow,

unmarked by man, so virgin white.

Bits of blue, like best porcelain,

what a glorious, breathless sight.

Now the sea of grey-green marble,

stretching as far as the eye can see.

Big ships, a lighthouse in model size,

huge waves, like ripples in the sea.

If all could fly, above God's earth just once,

to see ourselves as God us does see.

Humility would make us pray, with joy,

thank you God for noticing me.

We land at last, land flashes past,

the doors open on man's world again.

Strange how quiet and thankful we feel,

after our moment near God, in an aeroplane.

Ulster's Shame

The old red brick houses,

the new office blocks as well.

The wee shop on the corner,

the chain stores, all a story tell.

The empty streets, the broken glass,

the vacant car-parks, the crumbling halls.

The smoke spirals on the skyline,

the blood stained footpaths and bullet spattered walls.

Black bands on many wounded,

for fathers dead, for widows grief.

Sightless eyes, and faces scarred,

no rest from pain, or fear relief.

Whose screams do I hear at the midnight hour,

whose terror do I see in whose eyes,

who is right, who is wrong, who is weak, who is strong?

What matters is the depth of God's sighs.

Only He can wipe out our guilt,

only He, the blood stains can oblate.

Oh, the shame, oh the shame, oh the crying shame,

Ulster's shame is lying at our feet.

The Terror and the Tears

The night is dark, the doors are shut,

and we are again here on our own.

My child and I in terror lie,

in the bedroom of our home.

Every sound of gates that squeak,

every car that stops outside.

Every sudden crack or crunch we hear,

makes fear and terror in us ride.

Why do our hearts break this way,

why do we live in tears and dread?

What crime committed by us, you say,

why should others wish us dead?

No crime have we been guilty of,

no hurt, no pain, was caused by we.

But my husband risks his life each night,

and ours. Why? Because he's in the R.U.C.*

Yes, loyal to our country's cause,

to Queen and country, gives his life.

Because of this, evildoers all,

destroy the minds of his child and wife.

You, who are on the evildoer's side,

remember, our God both sees and hears.

The horrors you do, the deaths you cause,

you shall one day know the terror, and shed

tears.

Nonsense Rhyme

Did you ever see an elephant in pyjamas?

Did you ever see a jackal in a coat?

Did you ever see an adder in a bikini?

Did you ever see a giraffe with a scarf around his throat?

Did you ever see a panther in white sandals?

Did you ever see a chimpanzee with short pants and a vest?

Did you ever see an ape with medals on his chest?

Did you ever see a hippopotamus in a corset?

Did you ever see a tiger drinking tea?

If you ever, really, truly ever did see any of these things,

then you're twice as daft, no, thrice as daft as me.

The Brownie Pack

My Brownie Pack is the apple of my eye,

I'll mention each girl separately, to tell the reason why.

First there is my Robin, Edith is her name,

she's first class in playing in any Brownie game.

Second is First Topper, Melanie is her name,

she's attentive, willing, and gentle just the same

Second Topper Lorna is a tomboy, but likes to learn,

she's apt to be noisy, but good merits she will earn.

Then Jennifer, she is our little mother hen,

she likes to talk, and talk and talk, but we love her just the same.

Then Sharon, one of three sisters, is happy with her lot,

she is jolly, ginger, and alert, and always on the dot.

37

Catherine our ballerina, is pretty, quiet and petite,

she's a dainty Pixie, on her Pixie feet.

Helen is a Leprechaun, is full of beans and spice,

she's full of tomboy tricks, and really very nice.

Sandra is affectionate, and is sorry if she does wrong,

she is a little rascal, with an angel's song.

Ruth is another tomboy, pretty and full of fun,

she's always in the middle, of each game begun.

Beverly bites her hair, and pretends to be shy,

she's really a little devil, in the quiet bye and bye.

Gillian, our wee Goldilocks, with golden curls affray,

she's small, she's cute, she's a Brownie Elf, I'd say.

Naomi is clever with needle and with thread,

she's quiet, works hard, and thinks a lot instead.

Gina is a worrier, and takes things to heart,

she is anxious to earn merits, right from the start.

Lorraine is a little lazy, I'm sorry to say,

she'll earn no badges, she would rather play.

Elaine is tall and anxious, much to learn,

she'll go far in Guides, and many badges earn.

We have another Gillian, who is really shy,

but I believe she likes the boys, and is lively on the sly.

Alison, is a lively lass, she is a little pale,

but likes to eat lollipops, when we have a sale.

Lauren is a plump wee armful of Irish love,

she also likes to eat sweet things, but always on the move.

They are all my Brownie Pack, they mean a lot to me,

I love each and every one, God grant that they love me.

The Antrim Coast Road

(Larne to Waterfoot)

The Coast Road in Antrim,

I heard even Yankees say,

has a special magic quality,

as it winds from bay to bay.

The part which I know by heart,

since I was just a tiny tot,

is that bit that leaves north of Larne,

and winds its way to Waterfoot.

When leaving Larne,

cliffs to the left, sea and rocks hugging your right,

two miles more of rocky coast,

then the Devil's Churn is in your sight.

Just round the bend from Devil's Churn,

where rock snared sea e'er pounds,

a lazy looking village, a sandy beach,

the Drains Bay bungalows the sand surrounds.

Next leafy woods and gate guarding lodges,

to the left at the gates of Cairndhu,

the Lady Dixon's grand manor and grounds,

are very pleasant to our view.

Onward ever onward,

to nature's sculptured head,

the great man's face our headland,

known to all as Ballygally Head.

Now an always windy place,

yes, even on a summer's day,

a sandy beach, a castle's ruins,

what of Ulster's history it could say.

We sweep along to the Halfway House,

to a tavern of great renown,

halfway from wee higgledy Glenarm,

halfway from dear Larne town.

Now the land lies gentler to the left,

than it had ever done before,

the bays get rocky, the hillside green,

no sandy bays for sure.

Now great white cliffs which overhang,

dangerously above your head,

then nature's 'Mad Man's' window on the shore,

where many a life ended it's said.

Here we must be careful now,

here weather and sea are boss,

landslides down, and giant stones,

across the road into the sea oft toss.

We safely pass and wind at last,

to wee Glenarm in a shough*,

with white faced rocks about the shore,

we reach the outskirts of Carnlough.

The lands now easier to our sight,

and the coastline caresses the sea,

the grass grows greener, hedges high,

then we reach the surfing sea.

Along the winding road for miles,

the hills and dales seem mute,

no more villages or towns until,

we at last reach Waterfoot.

Here the rocks are dusty grey,

and we see the rock grey homes,

the bleakness is so pronounced,

no charm to render lyrical poems.

But a wee road to the west,

winds past cote to the glen,

to Glenariff of the Waterfalls,

the Great God's tears to startle mortal man.

Yes, this is my part of our Coast Road,

manmade with tears and sweaty brow,

when the potato famine came,

to our once blessed Isle, it's history now.

So someday soon just take the time,

to travel this road and glade,

give praise to men so long ago,

for the magic that they made.

The Old, Old Man

Come in me lad, sit down a while,

and listen to my tale,

an' keep an old man company,

afore I end up in jail.

Do ye see this wee house o' mine?

Not much to see, ye say.

Well, it's all I've ever had,

and it's here I mean to stay.

The man frae* the City Hall came in,

said I'd have to move no less.

This house is just a slum,' said he,

I was hindering the City's progress.

I fair lashed him wa'* me tongue,

to come into my home and scorn,

all the precious memories,

I've had here since I was born.

I was just seventeen when I got wed,

and brought Bessie here to stay.

A fine wee wife and three fine sons,

scattered o'er this world today.

Bessie's been gone now eighteen years,

and I vowed I'd wait for her here.

Sure if I move she'd not find me,

when the good Lord called me near.

Tomorrow the bulldozers come,

to knock down this old slum!!

Sure, ye'd think the Council men,

could understand this is my home.

Oh! Oh Bessie, ye've* come, ye're* here,

Oh my dear lass at last ye're come.

Now I'll leave this dear wee house,

for my Bessie is taking me home.

I was the lad in this tale,

watched the old man lie back in his chair.

I shed a tear as the old man died,

and the good Lord answered his prayer.

My Wee Grandchild

Christine Joanne is the name of my own grandchild,

with a twinkling eye and a devastating smile.

A chubby little bundle of love is she to me,

only she can unlock my heart, only she has the key.

Born on the seventeenth of December in 1971,

near the birth date of our God's own son.

May our good Lord guide and keep her all her day,

may she always remember Grannie when she kneels down to pray.

Guide her little steps, dear God along the stony ground,

and thank you Lord for the love in her that I've found.

The Unholy War

Has Armageddon started on its' way?

Just look around and hear what the Good Book say.

Read Revelations, and then just cast an eye,

oh, Prince of Peace, please come from out the sky.

The Good Book say brother blood by brother shed,

Father's heart, by son shall be bled.

Daughter's hand shall mothers heart sharp sting,

no baby to a mother shall longer cling.

Famine, pestilence, hate, war and flood,

they still cry Crucify, Crucify as they did before.

All parts of Earth shall cry out for its blood,

then weep and wail and His love ignore.

Turn ye back to God, Satan's children,

repent while you can.

Forsake the ways of Lucifer,

acclaim the Son of Man.

Forgive them Lord, only you can and will,

has Armageddon now begun, with each blood stained kill.

Look ye to the skies, the moon is red with blood,

remember brethren, fire this time, not flood.

The Lite Bite and Takeaway

The Lite Bite and Takeaway,

is our favourite place of work.

We gather there each morning,

and our duties do not shirk.

Ethel is our leading light,

and her head is nearly turned.

For every time she's out of sight,

at least one of us is burned.

We make our chips and pots of soup,

with love and charm and grace!!

We place our pies with simple pride,

to eat and toast, as does our face.

Our bacon, eggs and sausages are great,

our tea and coffee, *tres* supreme.

Our cream puffs, tarts, and pancakes,

are really from a dream.

Our sandwiches are varied,

our scones buttered sure to please.

With jams of many flavours,

Oh joy! Our farmhouse teas.

We are a pleasant mixture,

of young and not so very old.

But we work together very well,

until all our wares are sold.

So 'here's to our Lite Bite',

to our 'Carry Out' as well.

Here's to our Ethel and Doris,

to one and all, a Happy, very happy, Noel.

The Culinary Cuties Freak Out

The Culinary Cuties of the Lite Bite,

had a Christmas do in the Strangford Arms.

All arrived early dressed in their finery,

each showing many different types of charms.

All were soon seated at the dinner table,

melon well chilled and drinks for a start.

After some chattering and sipping of beverage,

we settled down to eat with merry heart.

We partook of our turkey, potatoes, greens and sauce,

soon devoured with relish and with speed.

Then lovely trifle with lots of cream on top,

and a lovely cup of coffee, just what we need.

Now the table's cleared and the band starts to play,

special requests the order of the day.

We send our waitress with our list of tunes,

and hear our names mentioned before they play.

Ethel is a jive fiend, skirts and legs a-flying,

Elsie likes to rock and roll it would seem.

Marion with her cowboy look swings a merry hip,

Mandy does a twist that causes us to scream.

Little Maggie two-steps as if she's really with it,

Wee May tries a waltz with a determined step.

Carol tries a foxtrot with a-one, a-two, a- three,

Gail does her sexy wriggle, for she's really hip.

Jenny does a blushing act watching all the boys,

Mae tries all there is to get right in the mood.

Martha does a trip of the light fantastic,

So we are all set to really have it good.

Lorna and Kathy, our two guests dance quite well,

giggling and laughing, and joking all the while.

Soon our night is over, and it's time to go,

say Good-night and off home to bed, so smile.

Our dinner dance was an evening of great fun,

so 'Here's to the Culinary Cuttles, so Good Cheer'.

So save up your pennies and your pounds for next time,

Toast to our Christmas Do, and with happiness on to our next New Year.

Pleasurable Pastime

You would never guess in a hundred years,

how at present I am passing my free time.

With an occupation so full of expectation,

that even the commonplace can seem sublime.

With Lilian and Bet, my best workmates yet,

our nimble fingers make up Christmas laughter.

The packages we make, dear Santa Claus will take,

to give to many children, joy hereafter.

We sit in 'Our Grotto', 'Keep busy' is our motto,

packing up our presents, by the score.

Books and games and toys, for happy girls and boys,

to work with so much joy, who could wish for more.

With Bob and Eve to guide us, and necessities provided us,

the job is truly fun and really a pleasure.

So good luck to 'Our Centre' and Mr Hanivan, our mentor,

with plenty fun and food, and Christmas Leisure.

Really!!!

I sat in my wee cashier box,

selling tickets to Santa's cave,

and as often in such a job as this,

I find not so queer, as how folk behave.

A mother comes with her five year old son,

she pays for a ticket for her 'wee John '.

He, half laughing, half sobbing, in fear wee soul,

'Come John,' says she, 'No, Ma!! I wanta* go home.'

'Now! You come on. I tell you, you hear!!

Get a present, and a photo to please your mom.

I'll shake you, you silly bad, bad boy.'

'Oh, Ma! I'm feart*. I wanna go home!'

'You are comin' in, and ye'll sit on Santa's knee,

an' ye're getting a gift, yes you are!'

'Ma, I'm feart, you go in, I'll wait'

'You are coming in, or you'll get what for!'

She drags him past the puppet shows,

Nursery rhyme land, just good clean fun.

'Look John, Little Miss Muffett, what did she do son?'

'I don't know Ma, I wanna go home'.

'Look John, 4 & 20 blackbirds, see the big pie.

Oh, look John, Jack Horner pulling out a Plum.

He put in his thumb, son, what did he do, son?'

'I don 't know Mammy, I want to go home.'

'You are going to 'Smack, smack, smack.

You are getting a gift, and a photo for your Da.

'Smack, smack, you silly wee boy!!'

'Oh no, Ma, I wanna go home. Oh! Ah! Aaah!'

So she drags the poor wee lad around,

then in to see Santa in his cave.

Boy screams and runs off down the mall,

'Wait till I get you. You'll behave'.

Along the mall the screams rang out,

'You've showed me up, you!'

You wee besom.' John 's Ma gave him a mighty clout.

'Just wait 'til I get you home'.

'I don't want to go home Mammy.

I don't want to go home. Ma! Ma! Ma! It's only a joke'.

I sat in my box and pondered a while.

Really! There is not so strange as folk.

My Vibrating Vertebrae

I limped into the Casualty Unit,

propped myself against the desk.

Sister-in-Charge got out a form,

and many questions of me did ask.

My name, address, where I worked,

the number of my 'phone, my Doctor's name.

Then at last, why was I here,

and where did I feel the pain.

I explained my fall, my back hurt,

soon Doctor Murphy came to me.

His hands were cold, his manner kind,

and my Xrays he wished to see.

So off I stumbled to the Xray unit,

undressed and donned a robe, so cold.

Into the Xray room I padded, bare feet,

onto the couch I climbed as I was told.

Several 'pictures' of my Spinal Column,

then I dressed again in great haste.

I felt like a 'Stripper' by this time,

take my 'pictures', felt wan and chaste.

Back to Outpatients for another test,

back to see doctor and gentle nurse.

My temperature was soaring high,

so Nurse took both temp and pulse.

Plenty of rest, no heavy lifts,

painkillers to take, when hurt was strong.

So out I stagger, and back to work,

to be with my mates where I belong.

Second Chance

At fifty-two I'm back at school,

and hoping to store up knowledge.

I am on a crash course for business gen,

and go to Newtownards Technical College.

We go in the door, 'Good morning, all',

then turn down to the right.

We enter the first room, and meet our mates,

not a teenager in sight.

All are over twenty one, ahem!

that's all we're prepared to confess.

Hope to gain knowledge, like our kids,

'O' levels we all want, no less!

We type our letters, A S D F. We do our Pitmans script with glee.

We learn our tables, do our sums,

swat verbs, nouns, and do a spelling bee.

Office practice is on open book,

Book-keeping now, more than a name.

We love our teachers, yes, every one,

God give them patience and keep them sane.

Panic

The small figure, ran a wild semi-blind race.

He was roared at by the trees, jeered at by the wind,

blinded by the rain, bombarding his little face.

Hobbled by the unevenness of the stony ground,

panic tasted bitter on his lips. Please God, I'll be good, keep me safe.

Really good, let me be homeward bound.

A light, thank you God in heaven sent rosy light.

He scrambled towards the golden glow.

A door, an open door. Martha, his mother looks into the night.

Mammy, I'm here, I'm home I'm cold, so very, very cold.

Her arms reached out, a rug, a warm red rug

Was placed about his shoulders, the shivering shoulders of on 8 year
old.

A mug, a mug of cocoa, hot and sweet.

The spoon still in the mug poked his eye.

71

The warmth from the log fire claimed his feet

Safe now he'd never slip out at night to roam.

Silly, dropping his torch, his cap, he'd lost his cap.

That owl, that almost human screeching owl.

Oh, I am glad, so very glad to be home.

Middle-aged Love

Rushing for the bus, hopping up the steps.

Sitting on the edge of seat, heart beating fast.

Tidying my hair, then powdering my nose

Looking in pocket mirror, wide-eyed and aghast.

Would I be late 'Oh, please, please no'.

Would I like my, as yet unseen, boy?

Would my new love learn to love me?

Oh! My heart fairly jumps with Joy.

Here is my stop, clutching bag, stepping down.

Is he really in this enormous building, waiting?

My cheeks flushing, my hands atremble.

Breathing fast, my nerves agitating.

A pretty lady welcoming me with a smile.

Showing me to the room, my new love occupies.

At last. at long last I would see.

The 'boy' of my dreams with my own eyes.

He is handsome, he is blonde and fair skinned.

His very beauty makes my heart go wild.

He raises his right hand, touches his eyes.

Oh yes, I do love him, my own, my beautiful first grandchild.

Lilian

So quick of step and sharp of tongue,

so tall, so slim of waist.

Clothes well groomed and tidy hair,

it's plain to see she's got good taste.

Grey of eye, which turns to charcoal,

when anger bursts within her breast.

Dilating nostrils like a thoroughbred,

arms flailing like a windmill in distress.

Her hair is grey? No, not quite! Fair.

Yes, fair, a sandy fair, a strawberry blonde.

Of course, a strawberry blonde with freckles.

Pale of lip, pale of cheek, and gay aplomb.

So cool at times, yes, almost aloof,

but really in search of love, yes affection.

No matter how hard she tries to guide us,

we all move in our sweet direction.

With her many bits of worldly knowledge,

gained as she travelled both near and far.

The army life gives itchy feet, I know,

it keeps her travelling with or without a car.

So tall of stature, so long of limb,

so quick of tongue, so sharp of wit.

Generating vitality with arms gesticulating,

but underneath it all, she is quite nice with it.

The Operation

He stood, the man so stern of face.

White-light glinting on the instrument,

with which the operation he'd perform on me.

My teeth were chattering, my soul in torment.

A local anaesthetic which he'd prepared.

I trembled as the man I paley* faced.

Sharp pain, oh! Another, a tear I shed.

As for vanity's sake, my ears were pierced.

Tender to Touch

A dear wee man with silver hair,

entered our shop one very cold day.

A bottle of 'Stomach Cure' was his wish,

we had a well-known brand on display.

He bought it, and gently touched his tum,

'Here is where I hurt, so I will try,

this remedy you have given to me.

I'll let you know if it works. Goodbye.'

Three weeks passed e'er he returned,

then in he bounced his face aglow.

'Hello girls, you all look well,

I've returned as promised to let you know'.

'Since I used your tummy-trouble cure,

I'm well and fine and quite all right.

Now I've got no pain at all,

'cos I rubbed it on my tum each night'.

I was aghast, I couldn't answer.

It was two teaspoons in water I recall,

to be swallowed before bedtime daily.

It was not a tummy rub at all.

So Hope and Health, and now simple faith,

are on our shelves for us to sell.

I love my work, especially the folks,

whom we endeavour to keep fit and well.

The Birth of a Business

There is a brand new business just opened in Conway Square,

'Take Five' is what we call it, it provides such wondrous fare.

Just call in and see us, and you will surely agree,

that our home baked scones and pastries are lovely with our tea.

Our three young bakers, Deborah, Sharon, and Lilian as well,

are all pretty nifty pastry cooks, this truthfully I tell.

Karen is our Cutie, still a novice in the trade of food,

but she is learning fast, and chats up the likely lads real good.

Hilary handles the cash flow, and pours out coffee and tea,

then Jack, poor Jack the only male, a tormented soul is he.

Jack, we need more milk. The fuses need repairing. Have we more
eggs?

Poor man, he's nearly up the wall and falling off his legs.

Keeping us all in order, with her face in an excited glow,

is Rene, our wee guiding light, she simply can't go slow.

Including me, I'm Mae by name, there are ten of us in all,

So 'Take Five' and make our restaurant your first port of call.

Thank You Toronto

Way up on the Huntly Road,

two friends of ours do dwell.

Two kind and happy people,

of whose hospitality I now tell.

They welcomed us after many years,

in true Canadian style,

with 'Come on in' and 'You're Welcome',

so sit down for a while.

They took us to their cottage,

even gave up to us their bed.

They wined us and they dined us,

and over the country with us sped.

When we go back to Ireland,

many a tear will surely flow.

The memories and the friendships,

back with us will truly go.

So to Olga and to Robert,

our prayers and love will stay.

May we meet again quite soon,

on a not too far off day.

Miss H

(Miss Hamilton)

About five foot two, or is it three,

head held high and quick of step.

An hourglass figure, trim in dress,

a grim picture, Oh no! Our Miss H is hep*.

Hair piled high, grey eyes flashing,

full of purpose with a Job to do.

Quick chat to staff, sets wheels a-rolling,

all ready to face a challenge new.

Soft pale cheeks, lightly powdered high cheek bones,

dark wavy hair, eyelashes long gleaming in health.

Quick of tongue in reproof but soft in sympathy,

as I have cause to know myself.

When hair let down to shoulder length,

a dozen years flee and she is young again.

85

Her smile is quick to ease your fear,

her hands are fast to ease your pain.

Although she doesn't tell a soul,

she has a voice that is sweet in song.

So hear my word portrait of your Chief Personnel,

may her reign in Woolco be very, very long.

Woolcos

I enter Woolcos to work each day,

with a sense of verve and of joy.

You see I work in a treasure trove,

of food, clothes, cosmetics, and almost every toy.

I meet up with my working friends,

we have a chat, and a little snack.

A wonderful beginning to any day,

a smile, a welcome, it's great to be back.

The bosses are all quite handsome,

well, nearly all to tell the truth.

If you do your work and be fair,

they don't offer much reproof.

It is especially exciting,

just before Christmas time. Oh boy!

A free Christmas dinner, served by,

all those handsome bosses. Great joy!

We really do appreciate,

a happy atmosphere at work.

It makes so much difference to us,

poor souls, so we do not shirk.

God speed to all my workmates,

to our dishy bosses great praise.

Perhaps, just perhaps, this poem of joy,

will get us all (yes all) a raise.

My Daughter

There was a brand new venture started on the street of Shiralee,

it was started by my daughter, with a little help from me.

She was the youngest qualified driving instructor at the age of
twenty-one,

it was a dream come true for her as independent she'd become.

It was the eleventh of September nineteen eighty four,

when she set off with her first learner from this front door.

The first three days, the pupils were eleven,

the next three really busied up, there were twenty-seven.

She loves her job and the joy it brings,

God give her the health to achieve great things.

The Women's Rural

We meet seven times a year on the cold dark nights,

in our own wee village hall under its friendly lights.

We have learned so many things, to cook, to sew, to make,

painting on silk, arranging flowers, and even how to bake.

Young models on parade in wedding gowns, some fashioned old, some new,

we've had talks on holidays with photographs to view.

We've heard tales of smuggling in distant days of yore,

and conservation grasslands for ducks from a frozen shore.

Aromatherapy, massage, and taking care of feet,

we've even learned about supper snacks, which really were a treat.

We've had our wee raffles to add just a little spice,

our bingo nights are favourite, our concerts really nice.

Our little chats over cakes and cups of tea,

entertained many friends from another rural community.

And who are we who seek friendships and never to be cruel?

We are very proud to be known as the Women's Rural.

Life!!!

So much pain, for us,

so little pleasure.

Are we just playthings,

for the Devil's leisure?

You give us a penny,

then come back for a pound.

You give us a smile,

then slap us to the ground.

You give us a kiss,

then slap us in the face.

Oh, Satan! Satan! Are you,

master of the human race?

Oh, my Jehovah,

Beloved of my heart,

Help us!! Mercy!!

Don't let us be torn apart.

Reach out your hand,

and help us to our feet.

Embrace us to your heart,

and make our life sweet.

Don't, my God, pray don't,

let the Devil win.

Don't let him torment Innocents,

for those who live in sin

The Lover

The wheelchair rested on a grassy bank,

and there beneath a near exhausted tree,

my lady breathed a harsh and swollen sigh.

Limply she rested, her labours all but done.

Her spirit shrank from long embattlement,

her mind sustained no bitterness or wrath.

She only prayed that soon her love would come,

with subtle remedies to soothe her path.

The shadows lengthened and a soothing breeze.

induced her soon to dream as died the day.

A squirrel scampered past her icy toe.

She made no move to hinder it in play.

At last she saw her lover from afar,

anticipation caused her heart to fastly beat.

He came to her between the Cypress trees,

his heavy cloak swept silent o'er her feet.

She raised her eyes to look Into his face,

though shadows hide his features from her gaze.

She recognised the firmness of his touch,

she knew the wisdom of his ancient ways.

The doctor came before the sun had gone,

but found in her now, no sign of breath.

Her lover's arms held her in cold embrace.

Her lover's name, as always, was called death.

Explanations of words marked*

Page 9

fadge*

Traditional Ulster & Scottish Potato Bread or Potato Cake

Page 19 & 23

nae* & Nae*

Ulster/Scots Dialect meaning 'no' as in 'no way'

Page 18

braw*

Ulster/Scots Dialect meaning 'Bonny', 'Handsome' or 'Lovely'

Page 23

ain*

Ulster/Scots Dialect meaning 'own' as in 'my own'

faither*

Ulster/Scots Dialect meaning 'Father'

Page 24

farls*

Ulster/Scots 'Soda Bread' usually round and divided into quarters

Page 34

R.U.C.*

Royal Ulster Constabulary, now called the

PSNI - Police Service of Northern Ireland

Page 44

shough*

Ulster/Scots Dialect meaning 'Roadside Drainage Ditch'

Page 48

wa'*

Ulster/Scots Dialect meaning 'with' as in 'with my tongue'

Page 49

ye've*

Ulster/Scots Dialect meaning 'You've' as in 'You've come'

ye're*

Ulster/Scots Dialect meaning 'You're' as in 'You're Here'

Page 63

wanta*

Ulster/Scots Dialect meaning 'want to'

feart*

Ulster/Scots Dialect meaning ''afraid' or 'fearful'

Page 14

Fenian*

Someone who belonged to or supported the Irish Republican Army (IRA), who were an illegal operation in Ulster (Northern Ireland)

Page 47

Frae*

Ulster/Scots Dialect meaning 'from'

Page 77

paley*

Ulster/Scots Dialect meaning 'Pale' as in 'pale faced'

Page 14

Prod*

Protestant

hep*

'Hip' as in 'she's hip' (1970's 'Hippie' style term meaning 'trendy')

- END -

Printed in Great Britain
by Amazon

71714502R00068